Note to Self

Love,

Gigi Roundtree

Kerri,

Thank you for your
support! Appreciate you
Queen!

♡,
Gigi

Dear YOU,

I got you!

Love,

Me

Dedicated to My Heartbeats
Will, Brianna and Elijah

Thank you for always being my motivation and believing in my dreams!

Dear Self,

Do not be bothered about the world's perception of you. Why do you base your worth on what the world believes is its concept of beauty? The world can't even make up its mind on what beauty truly is. Its concepts are not stable and are constantly changing. Instead of validating yourself by what the world thinks is en vogue at the moment, base your self worth and value on something real. Character is what really defines you, your value and how you matter in today's world. Beauty is fleeting but a good character is everlasting.

Love,
Self.

Dear Self,

Life can be a hard pill to swallow. You might feel consumed with regrets, failures, and insecurities daily. You might have experienced heartbreak, loss, jealousy, betrayal and bad memories. These things can plague you deeply, thereby controlling your actions and emotions. You might wish you could erase and take them back, but what is done is done. Do not allow yourself to get overwhelmed by these situations which you have no control over. You might not be able to take it back but there are some aspects of the situation you can change. When deciding to make a change, understand why you are making these changes. Accept that there are some things which cannot be changed and change the things which you refuse to accept.

Love,
Self.

Dear Self,

You shouldn't have to sacrifice your happiness for the sake of others. Not everyone is an appropriate match for you. If someone makes you feel bad about yourself, and doesn't share your interests, it's perfectly fine to put that relationship on the back burner. Maybe you were close at one time, but people change and grow in different directions. This doesn't mean there's something wrong with either of you. If someone in your life is no longer good for you, it's okay to let them go.

Love,

Self.

Dear Self,

Challenges are inevitable regardless of the level of your intelligence. Any challenge that you successfully address strengthens your ability to overcome future challenges, as it will not stop coming. So, when you overcome a despairing moment, brace up for the next one. The difficulties are not meant to break you, but to improve your character and build your resilience. Shun unproductive thoughts, accept that it is not unusual to go through challenges in life and resolve to overcome it. Work positively through your ideas and come up with viable solutions to address the issues.

Love,
Self.

Dear Self,

You have been beaten down so many times, you find it difficult to get up once again. You are tired and wondering if there is a point to anything. But there is a point, and as long as you are living, you have a purpose. You might not see it now but in time, it will manifest. Too many people are unhappy because they do not accept the things or circumstances that they cannot change or have no control over. Stay strong.

Love,
Self.

Dear Self,

There might be times when your life feels torn apart and you are not sure how to begin putting the pieces back together. The things which mattered to you might disappear in an instant, and you realize you have no power to control certain things or situations. You need to always remember that some things are out of your control, and you don't have the answers to everything. Trying hard to find the answers to difficult questions in the face of traumatic events only blocks the answers from arising naturally in their own due time.

Love,
Self.

Dear Self,

Make conscious choices based on who you are and what you want. It's easier to set goals when you know where you're headed. You are wasting time going around in circles, living life through trial and error situations - which end up making you feel confused and unfulfilled. Right now, what you are doing is reacting to whatever life throws at you. Establish who you are, and it will be easier to get motivated. Know the best course to take in reaching your desired future.

Love,

Self.

Dear Self,

Don't get distracted by yesterday's problems and tomorrow's worries. It will be hard to stay strong when all you think about is what happened in the past, or predicting what horrible things you will face tomorrow. Leave all that for a minute and focus on what's going on around you. Enjoy this moment and stop worrying about what tomorrow might bring.

Love,

Self.

Dear Self,

Be patient with yourself, take your journey step-by-step, and enjoy how life unravels for you. You miss out on so much by beating yourself up when things do not go as planned. Patience is key to discovering the beauty of the mystery that every moment brings to you. If you fail, evaluate your mistakes, and try again. Don't allow yourself to get stuck in the same situations. There is a solution to every problem, remember that.

Love,

Self.

Dear Self,

Do not allow your emotions to take control of your decisions. When your emotions take over, you can't battle it with reasoning. Too many times this path takes you to regret. To fight toxic emotions - empty your mind. Sometimes you may forget that you are the one in charge of your thoughts. Simply put, the only way to fight against feeling bad about yourself is by finding ways to feel good about yourself.

Love,

Self.

Dear Self,

If you don't want to keep feeling stuck and depressed, you have to endeavor to grow as a person. Growth takes a commitment to improving every aspect of your life. When you don't improve upon yourself, you risk becoming obsolete. The world is constantly moving forward and it is crucial for you to keep up with its changes. If you don't keep up, you will get left behind. Don't rush to do something, as doing something too fast will only overwhelm you. Improvements should be made one at a time, as mastery takes time.

Love,
Self.

Dear Self,

The world is in need of what you alone can offer. You are unique and special, there is no other or better you, than you. There is a purpose you were created and you alone are instrumental in discovering it. Purpose encourages vision, and vision drives your passion - which in turn leads you to your desired future. Success.

Love,
Self.

Dear Self,

Life is filled with choices. The choices you make will determine your experiences and the eventual outcome of your life. Will you take charge and make the necessary changes - that will lead you to your desired, favorable outcome? Or will you wait for your fate to be determined by someone else? Become the creator of your destiny by actively responding to situations. Try out new ideas when you are faced with a challenge and persevere until you get your desired outcome. When you choose to be the creator of your fate, you accept responsibility and your goals will be achieved.

Love,
Self.

Dear Self,

As an adult, you are expected to take full responsibility and acknowledgment of your actions. Guilt and blame are simply avenues used to evade challenges instead of responding to it head on. The time wasted shifting blame around will be better spent finding a solution to the issue. When you have a challenge, do not be tempted to shift blame onto others, or yourself. Seek a solution for it, instead of proclaiming judgement.

Love,
Self.

Dear Self,

There are different ways to approach setting and planning your goals, however, it is crucial to give attention to all parts of your life. Neglecting or ignoring any aspect of your life will result in some problems. The five areas which you should set your goals are; Spiritual, Family, Social, Physical, and Work. These five parts combine in making who you are. Failure to pay attention to any part will cause an imbalance - resulting in social, spiritual, physical and emotional problems. You can reach your desired goals only if you maintain a balance in all facets of your life.

Love,

Self.

Dear Self,

Life has many unexpected turns, twists and surprises that make it worthwhile. It is a journey of self-discovery. Many times in life, opportunities come in disguise as problems. When you are in challenging situations, don't see it as the end of life. See through the situation and understand the lessons from it, which will guide your steps in life. It is not a time to get consumed in self-pity, but an opportunity to seek your Creator for guidance, and work on being the best version of yourself.

Love,
Self.

Dear Self,

Pleasing everyone will only put you at a disadvantage. You can't put your own needs on the back burner and instead accommodate everyone else's. Agreeing to do things are not beneficial to your well-being. You need a certain amount of selfishness to maintain your personal boundaries. You are not doing anyone favors, least of all - yourself, when you try to please them at your own expense. Eventually, you will be respected for disagreeing with them. When you say, 'No,' it shows you have an opinion, a defined plan and a vision. You can only achieve your full potential when you put yourself first.

Love,
Self.

Dear Self,

Fear is the major culprit behind giving excuses. It can develop from lack of understanding or experience. Fear and self-confidence don't work together. When you lack confidence, you will fail to take actions that are necessary to achieve your goals. Consequently, giving you room for excuses to redeem yourself. Failure and unhappiness in your personal and professional life is your mistake that you have to learn from. Start accepting your mistakes and downfalls, and turn your life around by doing better next time. Grow through what you go through.

Love,
Self.

Dear Self,

See yourself in a positive light to enhance your self love, and compliment yourself. Daily affirmations will provide you an emotional boost, which will make you happy. But, you will have to strengthen the impact of that compliment by proving it to yourself. Find that happy state to spread to people around you.

Love,
Self.

Dear Self,

You have to learn to accept who you are. And the real you isn't the 'you' in your low moments. The real you is the 'you' who is ready to dust yourself off and forge ahead. Learning to accept yourself however you are is the real 'you'. Your true self is the 'you' who is working to turn your weakness to strength. You should not compare the negative views of yourselves with the unrealistic views of other people.

Love,

Self.

Dear Self,

Holding grudges against someone is doing harm to yourself, especially your health. Genuine forgiveness has the healing power to your soul; it has a way of making you find great relief, as the heaviness of heart is being lifted. Forgiveness doesn't mean that you condone what happened, but means that you're no longer interested in investing negative emotional energy in a particular person or situation. It helps you come to terms with your past experiences. And aids in ending your suffering, pain, anger, and resentment around the event. Forgiveness is the best gift you can give yourself.

Love,

Self.

Dear Self,

Life will always put you to test, pushing you to the edge of what seems impossible. It is necessary to upgrade your mental preparedness at this point to keep pressing on until you attain your goals and objectives. Do not succumb to the belief that the challenges are way beyond your capabilities and means. Don't forget that obstacles are just temporary roadblocks along your journey, strategically positioned to help you learn some life lessons and work on yourself. It is not a time to give up, but to persist and persevere till you reach your goal.

Love,
Self.

Dear Self,

You cannot move forward until you let go of the past. Doing this gives you the power to live freely in the present moment - where you have the choice to turn things around and decide the path you want to take. This choice cannot be found in the past. Only in the present moment. As great as the present moment is, it's important that you don't get stuck there either, but commit yourself to moving forward. In moving forward, acknowledge and accept the lessons that the past has given you and give yourself permission to start anew. Don't be afraid to start over as many times as necessary, in order to create the life you truly desire to live.

Love,

Self.

Dear Self,

Do not yield to the temptation of inconsistency. In the course of fighting to get what you want, do not get distracted. The fact that the immediate results from your actions are not evident, doesn't necessarily mean that you are in the wrong direction. The habit of consistency isn't about getting quick results, but entails making incremental progress and improvements over an extended period of time. Commit yourself with the right course of action, no matter how long it might seem to take, the results you seek will eventually come.

Love,

Self.

Dear Self,

Be assertive but don't make enemies out of it. Make your point without hurting the feelings of others, or becoming upset yourself. It is not unlikely to find yourself yielding to the temptation to act in passive and aggressive ways from time to time. But, make conscious efforts not to become a victim of such, which often results from lack of self-confidence, as it is an inappropriate way of interacting with others.

Love,

Self.

Dear Self,

Words that proceed from your mouth are powerful, as your mind literally goes in the direction of your words. It is almost impossible for you to shout, "I feel fantastic!" and still be depressed at the same time. What you say, or think, has the potential to either heal or harm you. A few verbal affirmations throughout the day leaves you high-spirited. Positive words have the power to transform you into a better individual. Make a personal choice to pass on positivity in your speech, and speak positively to yourself on daily basis.

Love,
Self.

Dear Self,

Happiness is a choice that can be determined by you alone. Your happiness is not dependent on anybody, anything, or any feeling, but you. When confronted with countless circumstances that life throws at you, take a hold of what you can control to bring about more happiness in your life. Determine what habits and behaviors you can change to open doors of happiness. Your set point for happiness is in your hands. Do not give anyone the power to dictate your moods. Your set point for happiness is in your hands. Take back control over your life.

Love,
Self.

Dear Self,

Negative thoughts have no basis in life; they are not real. Permitting such thoughts can become so automatic that you won't consider the possibility that it is not realistic. You have to watch what you think about the situations you find yourself in, as they have their way of complicating your experience of stress. Negative thoughts can blur your vision, and prevent you from seeing solutions that might exist to the problems you are facing. Look at the situation in a different way to displace distorted thinking, and replace them with more realistic thinking to work things out in your favor.

Love,
Self.

Dear Self,

Your mind needs nourishment just like the physical body, and one way to nourish your mind is through reading which also increases your wisdom. Nourishing your mind helps you nurture your spirit. Reading fills your mind with information that inspires you to move on. When you find yourself in the heat of a trying situation, make it of necessity to read stories of those who have gone through similar situations, and how they overcame it. It will raise your hope, give you a new and better perspective to the situation, and provide you new ways to face and deal with the challenges.

Love,
Self.

Dear Self,

Plan well to execute your goal. Proper planning helps you deal appropriately with unforeseen challenges that might arise in the future. In planning, give allowance for flexibility; don't be too rigid in your approach as there may be times you will have to adjust your laid down plan of action to a more realistic and workable approach. When certain activities lead you nowhere, change your course of action and maximize your efforts in the right direction.

Love,
Self.

Dear Self,

Have a clear picture of what you foresee about you, the kind of life you would love to live? Pen down your thoughts in full detail and clarity, especially the ones that concerns the key areas of your life such as your love life and relationships, career and contribution, wealth and lifestyle, health and wellbeing, learning and creativity, and soul or spirituality. Also, write down what you intend to do to help you become the person you visualized.

Writing down your goals increases your chances of becoming what you see of you in the picture, especially if you work towards it. Set a target and timeline to actualize your objectives from the break down of the main goals. The clearer your vision, the more motivation you will have towards making it a reality.

Love,

Self.

Dear Self,

The answer you seek is within, just stay calm and listen. You have to pay attention to that inner voice and do away with those friends that envelope you with negative energy, as they will do you no good if you truly want a healthy social circle. Seek for where and with whom you can find peace and stick with them, especially in your low moments. Your intuition will always give you the right direction if only you will succumb to its guidance.

Love,
Self.

Dear Self,

There are things that happen each day that you can feel good about, even on a typical bad day. Staying grateful for the good of the day will help you identify what went right from wrong. Think deeply to understand why things were allowed to happen and why you should feel good about it. You will be amazed with the results of appreciating things more as they happen. Remember we do not have bad days, only bad moments.

Love,

Self.

Dear Self,

Reaching for help when needed is not a sign of weakness, but an opportunity to have the burden on your shoulders lifted. Asking for help doesn't imply overstepping friendships, or appearing too needy, but a way of partaking in the gift of nature to share. Don't allow fear to get in the way of seeking for help, as it will only prevent you from getting necessary support, and weary you more. Your team of supporters are out there, willing to lend a helping hand. Reach out to them for help and you will be glad you did.

Love,
Self.

Dear Self,

Life comes with challenges in your professional and personal lives that can trigger your stress level. If changing the way you see things that upset, scare, or challenge you will make you happier, more confident, and less stressed, please step back and do it. Negative viewpoints can be worrying and energy-draining, affecting you both mentally and spiritually. Channel the energy into something more useful by changing the way you perceive your world. Remain positive no matter what life throws at you. Always shift your perspective of all situations to a more positive viewpoint to enhance your state of well-being.

Love,

Self.

Dear Self,

Toss things around and see the situation from a different dimension. You will understand that the current situation would be redefined based on your interpretation. Different views about a situation will help you see the need to be optimistic and become more positive with time. This practice will not only help you stay positive, but will help you feel better in the nearest future. Since tides always turn, stay calm and wait for the part that can help move you to the land of greatness.

Love,
Self.

Dear Self,

Never try to escape yourself, when life gets really tough as nothing is insurmountable so long as you work at it. Don't forget that there are many different paths up the same mountain. Be resilient enough to find your way to the top, because you possess the power to turn every "No" into a "Next." No matter the challenges life confronts you with, face it boldly to address the issue. Remember that there is always a solution to any problem.

Love,

Self.

Dear Self,

Change is inevitable in life, and it is necessary for your development. You should not entertain fear and anxiety in any way because you do not feel in control. Find ways to adapt as those changes come by being flexible. It will be too dangerous to refuse to move and take the right direction because of shame or embarrassment. It is important to note that when you cannot change your circumstances, you have to change yourself.

Love,

Self.

Dear Self,

You are totally responsible for your life. You must be ready to give account and take full responsibility for your decisions and actions (whether good or bad) when required. Never give away your control to events, people or circumstances. Loss of control over your life and loss of firm grip of your destiny, sets you on course for failure. Make no excuses for anything you do, or for anything that happens to you. Take full responsibility of your actions and take charge of your destiny.

Love,
Self.

Dear Self,

Knowing the reason for your existence, will enable you to bear almost any hurdle that comes along because you know where you are going. Purposeful living motivates you to hold on to your dreams. Your happiness in life is tied around achieving your dreams which can only come when you know your purpose for living and work towards it. Therefore, stay focused on the bigger picture when facing hardship as long as you are on the right course, push until you reach your goal and achieve great success in life.

Love,
Self.

Dear Self,

You can not be complacent with your condition in life. It is unwise to accept anything life presents you. Don't be afraid to make mistakes and fail. You can only progress in life when you make efforts to succeed. Your experiences can be the lessons you need to show you the right way to success, as it will help you become wiser. Never try to stop yourself from going in a bold new direction, if that is what you need to advance in life. Never try to stop yourself from starting afresh to get the right step.

Love,

Self.

Dear Self,

Change is the only permanent thing in life, and that includes your personal growth. Self improvement is not just about the physical, but about working on yourself to become a better version of You, from inside out. Life is about learning; life is about change. Constantly make self-conscious efforts to shed negative qualities you have acquired over the years. Instead imbibe better qualities which help you become a better You.

Love,
Self.

Dear Self,

You cannot force situations to soothe your desires, but you can force yourself to change to the form that can grow past those circumstances without getting damaged. Like a thread needing readjustment to pass through the eye of a needle. Find something to change about you, especially if it is getting in your way of progressing in life. Adjust to create the necessary change you need to enable you to overcome that particular situation. This may include changing your viewpoint or converting certain weaknesses into strengths, etc.

Love,
Self.

Dear Self,

Life comes with many challenges. Sometimes, these challenges come in various forms and in quick successions. Just when you thought that you have found peace after a turbulent period of time, you may be presented with another challenge worse than the former. If you are unprepared, you might find yourself drifting away from your life direction, or worse still, giving up on your life goals (the reason for your existence). Becoming a better You helps you manage your emotions as you go up life's ladder that leads to your goals. Focus on becoming a better person as you journey in pursuit of your life goals.

Love,

Self.

Dear Self,

The power to turn around things in your favor lives within you, right in your mind. You lose control of your life if you cannot take charge of your thoughts. What you permit in your thoughts affects your character, habits and situations. If you want a better outcome of your challenges in life, you have to become the master of your thoughts. Do not allow aimless thoughts and worries creep into your mind. Change your thoughts today to positively change your life and circumstances with lasting results.

Love,
Self.

Dear Self,

"What was my purpose of meeting this person?" … Some were meant to guide you on your life journey, others were meant for lessons to enable you to learn and become a better person. And others? Well we go on and think "wasted time"… Right?! Maybe they are around a season or two? Maybe for many seasons too long! Have an open-minded heart and be willing to learn from anyone and everyone because each and everyone you meet in your lifetime has a lesson to teach you. This is not to say you should drag them along even when they weigh you down on your path to self-fulfillment. No matter the age and the bad experience with certain people you meet, learn what needed to be learnt and move on.

Love,
Self.

Dear Self,

Don't underestimate the power of relationships. The type of people you choose to relate with can either make or break you. Build good supportive relationships with people who believe in your dreams, and lend their helping hands during your high and low moments. Stick with those that see great potentials in you and encourage you to help maximize them. Those who will make you are those you can trust, that inspire and motivate you to act and be the best you can be. Those who will break you discourage you from making positive moves, and deliberately put stumbling blocks on your way to success. When you find a meaningful relationship, invest in it to flourish. However, don't hesitate to let them go when they have played their roles in your life and are becoming your setbacks.

Love,
Self.

Dear Self,

The troubles of life did not come to consume you, but to unveil your inner strength. You may not know what you possess till circumstances stretch you beyond limit to utilize your strength to solve your problems. It is not a time to get broken and feel incapacitated. It is time to seek why you were going through such a distressing moment. It is a period to seek what you can do to become a better person and overcome the challenge. The troubles come for you at your weakest moments. You may never know your strengths till you are forced by circumstances to try something new.

Love,
Self.

Dear Self,

Don't be too quick to say, "I cannot" when you have not tried. Never be afraid to venture into something new that will be of benefit to you and humanity. If you have great ideas, put it to use. Don't let your ideas end without bringing it to life. Don't believe you don't have what it takes to achieve great things in life. Just give it a try and push a little harder to unlock those great potentials you never thought you had. Believe in yourself, and put in more efforts than the usual to discover more things you could do.

Love,
Self.

Dear Self,

No matter what people say about you, or how poorly they think of you, never doubt your capabilities. Rather, let it challenge you to bring out the best in you. Don't ever feel victimized by people's capabilities, their poor remarks about you or by their attainment. Avoid being around people that relegate you as worthless because they don't see what you can offer them in life. Never let them take advantage of you because of certain things they feel you cannot do, or not have. Strive to convert those limitations to capabilities to reveal your true worth. You are not worthless because of that position you find yourself. You too can make it and climb higher. You got this!

Love,

Self.

Dear Self,

You are bound to encounter fear, pain, doubt, and sometimes, failure in your endeavors to move farther than the usual. This is very normal because you have never given it a try. You are used to stopping at where you felt was your limit. But, the truth remains that you can achieve whatever you set your mind to if you work at it. You just have to keep trying even if you fail. When you move past your fear and pain, you will realize how much you can do to achieve whatever you want.

Love,
Self.

Dear Self,

There are many things you can do in life to be successful, but there is always one thing that you will be passionate about. Finding what you love is not always going to be an easy journey before the rewards start flooding in. Be ready to go through tough times, and suffer while putting yourself to test and perfection. Stay strong and consistent as long as you are on the right course. Allow your passion to be the force that drives you!

Love,
Self.

Dear Self,

In times of adversity, you know the kind of strengths and weaknesses you possess. This is because life comes with tests to reveal your present state of being... How you handle the situations show whether or not you pass the test. Your true strength lies in how you dealt with them. You are to grow in your strengths during distressing moments, and not get weaker in your weaknesses. When you overcome a challenge, you will be able to identify your strengths that enabled such victory. Always see troubles of life as moments to grow and add to your strengths.

Love,
Self.

Dear Self,

Don't live in torments of your past. The fact that things didn't go down well with you in the past, does not mean that it will always be that way. Don't limit yourself with those hurtful memories of the past. Shut your mind completely off the thoughts, and don't ruminate over them as they can discourage you from moving forward. Refuse to replay the ugly events in your head, no matter the temptation to fall back on it. Choose and make deliberate efforts to let go. You can make it if you let your past remain in the past.

Love,
Self.

Dear Self,

Don't spend the time you would have used to engage your mind on relevant things, like growing your ideas, to preoccupy it with thoughts of people that has hurt your feelings and emotions. It is okay to feel disappointed with them for their actions but don't dwell so much on it that it starts to affect your personal growth, especially when they do very little or nothing for you.

Love,
Self.

Dear Self,

You have the seed of greatness in you. The way you nurture it depends on how well you will thrive in life, and that is where your true happiness and satisfaction lies. You can not just settle for less than what you truly deserve. Don't resort to doing what visionless and purposeless people do, as it will leave you with a life of emptiness in the end. You can nurture the seed by reading self-help books, and investing your time and energy on your personal development. All these can be really demanding and stressful but you will have reasons to be thankful that you did later in life.

Love,
Self.

Dear Self,

Desist from using people's achievements to measure your level of greatness, as you are not the same by your life purpose. When you know your worth, you might even realize that you possess far more greater achievements. Our standards are an extension of our values. Your level of talent and potential are irrelevant if you're surrounded by people who don't help you realize it. Identify where you are and make further plans and efforts to be what you envisaged to be.

Love,
Self.

Dear Self,

There are many challenges you are bound to encounter on your journey called LIFE. Some days come with more frustrating challenges than the other. Some other days come with little or no challenges at all. No matter how frustrating they might seem, never give up. Keep fighting for the good till you win at the end. Do not quit when you have not reached your goal. No matter the number of times you failed, keep trying and what seemed hopeless will turn to glorious success. Most fail their way to success.

Love,
Self.

Dear Self,

The fact that you didn't get it right now, does not mean you cannot get it if you try again tomorrow. Don't limit yourself with those humiliating mistakes of the past. You can make it if you try again differently without repeating the same mistakes. Just do your best each time you try. I believe in you!

Love,

Self.

Dear Self,

Find balance in everything you do. Don't be too overzealous with work that some aspects of your life begin to suffer. Know what to be very serious about and what to take less seriously. Know when to loosen up a bit and have some fun. Do something exciting sometimes to keep your work and social life going. Enjoy yourself when it is required in order to improve the quality of your life. You need relaxation to stay mentally and physically fit for the job ahead. Finding balance in all aspect of our lives is key to happiness.

Love,
Self.

Dear Self,

It is very normal to feel tired, but misusing the word "tiredness" in order to run away from work is sign of laziness, especially when it becomes regular. It is okay to feel tired with mental exhaustion or low energy, and at some point you need to rest. Don't rest when you have bursts of energy that should have been used to get important things done. Get busy when you ought to and shun laziness to avoid setbacks in life.

Love,

Self.

Dear Self,

It is okay to slow down but not to quit, as you would be making things more difficult for you to get back and keep up the pace. The worst of all is that you might never be able to move forward again. When you feel too exhausted from life troubles, don't stop completely. It is okay to take one step at a time towards your goal, even if you have to drag your feet. The idea to quit starts from the mind. Before your body really becomes ready to quit, your MIND thought had long nursed the idea and quitted. Whenever the thought to quit gets the best of you, push your mind to move forward. It will help you push past the barrier that's in your way.

Love,

Self.

Dear Self,

There is a trick that always works in life... and that is smiling even in midst of a storm. This might seem ridiculous and difficult, but it helps! Your smile can attract beautiful things to brighten up your day. Keep smiling because it will help you see situations from a better viewpoint. A contagious smile can bring joy to everyone's day.

Love,
Self.

Dear Self,

It is not uncommon to get tired at the peak of heated battles. The winning team will be those that continue to fight till finish. It will be wiser to continue to push harder since you are almost at the finish line. It is just a matter of time and persistence before your life struggles finally come to an end. Exercise a little more patience and remain consistent, your reward is just one step ahead.

Love,
Self.

Dear Self,

Don't expect everyone one to like you even if you are the nicest person on earth. There are people that are always angry with themselves, but don't let that stop you from being GREAT. Don't occupy your head with worry trying to find what you have done to them, it is not your fault; they are just that way. Enjoy friendships with those that make you feel accepted and wanted. The positive energy around them will help you a lot.

Love,

Self.

Dear Self,

Anger and resentment can hinder you from progressing in life. When you becloud your mind with anger and resentment, you surround yourself with negative energy, which can have detrimental effect on you and people around you. There is no way you can have a positive life with a negative mind because the feeling will weigh you down. But forgiveness brings about physical, mental and emotional healing. Forgiveness brings peace into the mind, help you see the lessons to learn, and progress faster.

Love,
Self.

Dear Self,

You don't have to explain your words and actions if it is going to affect your self-esteem, especially when you know that they won't reason with you. Remain silent if you know that your thoughts and feelings mean nothing to them. Don't care too much about what they may think if you don't explain yourself. You may end up changing the way you act and come out of character. In this - you can lose your uniqueness and value, and become timid, consequently losing the voice to always air your opinion, just not to offend them.

Love,
Self.

Dear Self,

You need joy for your mental and physical well being. It will be foolhardy to allow anyone to take that away from you... for whatever reason. Learn not to take things to heart; if it belongs to you, it will stay; and if it doesn't, it will go; and, let it go. Learn to make yourself happy and joyous. Don't allow worry because of that situation. Don't allow depression because of what someone did or said to you. It is okay to feel bad... but don't let it hurt you for so long that it starts eating you up inside and preventing you from being amazing. The secret to finding true happiness lies within us!

Love,
Self.

Dear Self,

Don't worry yourself over what people say because of the actions you took to guide yourself from further hurt. You knew what you went through; only you understand that pain; you alone had your feelings hurt. If the actions you took were right and helped you get better, don't regret it; and nobody has the right to judge you because you were the one in pain - not them. Disassociate yourself from them and keep it moving!

Love,
Self.

Dear Self,

Almost everyone who talks about you, especially behind your back - lack something they feel you have. Care less about them, especially those that talk about you with hatred and resentment; it only shows their weakness (i.e they have a bitter life). Don't worry yourself trying to know what people say about you in your absence, you have more important things to do. The truth remains that people will always talk about you, good or bad. Just focus on working on yourself to be better than you are. Leave them to talk, that is the only job they have at hand.

Love,
Self.

Dear Self,

Don't always expect to get what you want. Sometimes, not getting what you want is for your own good. If it is meant for you, it will definitely be yours. Your inability to acquire what you want, might be to avert misfortune from happening to you. It could also have happened to make you divert your attention to something more beneficial, unknown to you. Don't always see what you couldn't get despite all you have put in as a problem, see it as an opportunity to do something different. You might find your blessings in doing that something different.

Love,

Self.

Dear Self,

Be careful when you find yourself boasting about your accomplishments, and start disrespecting others. Don't see yourself as superior to others because of fame. Don't become so arrogant that you start to lose yourself. Because, when failure in any form creeps into your life, it will affect you badly. Today you are successful, tomorrow might be their turn; shame will not allow you to face them tomorrow when you are no longer relevant. When success comes- always be willing to show others the way!

Love,

Self.

Dear Self,

Humility reveals your strength of character. When you are humble, you show modesty about your achievements and how well rooted you are in your values. Humility helps you focus on giving, not taking. Humility helps you listen to others, and not talk about yourself. Humility prevents you from feeling you have arrived, and help you realize that there is much more to learn and earn in life. With humility, you will stay focused and remain on track.

Love,
Self.

Dear Self,

Let past failures be in your past, or else they will start affecting the progress of the present. You start losing your confidence and self-worth if you permit thought of failures in your heart. When failures get to your heart, you become sad and depressed; you will start seeing negative things about life. Don't forget to learn from everything that happened to you, and that includes failures. Always fight to get back on your feet whenever you fall.

Love,
Self.

Dear Self,

These three things can ruin your life if you allow them to control you - instead of the other way round. Money controls you when you become rude and talk down on people because you feel you have more than someone else. Man (could be anyone) controls you when you begin to lose yourself to please them. When you allow what they say or do to change who you really are. Painful memories control you when you allow it to hinder you from moving forward because you always reflect on it. If you must make it in life watch three three things - Money, Man and painful Memories.

Love,
Self.

Dear Self,

Whenever you feel angry or provoked by anyone, don't be quick to use words or get physical; be slow to react. Breathing in and out will enable you take charge of the situation, and not for the situation to control your being. It will help you stay calm to the point that you no longer feel overwhelmed by the situation... sometimes we forget to think before we speak.

Love,
Self.

Dear Self,

You can do anything you put your mind to, even if it's "I can't". - depending on the strength of your faith and hope. When you become optimistic, your mind becomes open for you to see things you can do to become successful. But, when you cloud your mind with pessimism, even when the opportunities are right before you, you will not be able to see them because your senses are already engaged with the thoughts of impossibility.

Love,
Self.

Dear Self,

When you put smiles on people's faces, you will end up smiling irrespective of what you are going through. There is always this good feeling you get when you make people happy. It might not be money, it could be words of encouragement, it could be cracking simple jokes just to make the person laugh; so long as you make the person leave you feeling good. Don't let a day pass by without making someone smile at least, and you will be glad you did just that.

Love,
Self.

Dear Self,

Your sense of reasoning is usually not at its best when you are low spirited. Before making decisions, ensure that you are in total control of yourself which is usually in absence of worry and anxiety. Don't be quick to take decisions (especially those with lasting and costly effects) when you can wait till you are calm and in charge, or else you will live your entire life in regrets. Revisit the matter later and you will be happy you waited.

Love,
Self.

Dear Self,

It is not surprising to know that lies spread fast like wildfire than truth. When someone tells you something that seems like gossip, don't be quick to believe and judge! Most importantly - don't contribute. Listen and let it end there. If you must say it to someone else for whatever reason, verify the authenticity of that information before you "spread". Let's not waste time engaging in other people's gossip. However, if it is that important to spread the information, please verify.

Love,

Self.

Dear Self,

Live a life of contentment so that you don't drive yourself to things or places that will eventually kill you... just to get what you don't have. Obsession can make you do almost anything... be it right or wrong to get what you want, and usually it is something not right. Focus and do with what you have and grow from there.

Love,

Self.

Dear Self,

No matter how little you have, start from there. Where there is consistency, there is growth. Consistency is the key to breaking bad habits and forming good ones. Everything seems to flow better when there is CONSISTENCY.

Love,
Self.

Dear Self,

When it seems like all roads are blocked, use the power of your mind to find your own way. When life throws challenges upon challenges at you, use the power of your imagination to find your way through those challenges. Visualize your dream self as you shut your eyes. See yourself in that dream house, and all you desire in that vision. This will help you stay positive and remain hopeful. You will soon find your dream coming to reality just as you have imagined. Keep striving!

Love,
Self.

Dear Self,

It is not always about your money today, but about what you can offer without it. If your pocket is made empty today, your skill set should be able to fetch you wealth tomorrow. It is not about the size of your pocket, but on what you possess that can fetch you more money to add to what you have. Work on improving your skills. Work on acquiring more skills. You will find them useful tomorrow.

Love,

Self.

Dear Self,

Free yourself of that pain by letting your tears flow down your cheeks; it doesn't make you less of a man/woman. It is always good to cry at times... to help you feel relieved and take away that heaviness. Let those tears drop to take away the bitterness. Don't try to hold it back, let it out. As you let the tears out, let go of the burden. Let go the cause of the pain. Let the cause go with the tear drops, it will help you find clarity and peace.

Love,
Self.

Dear Self,

Don't engage in things that has little or no importance to you when you have more important things to do ahead of you. There is time constraint with life. You might be called upon to leave earth at anytime. So, while you still have breath in you, make best use of the opportunities before you to maximize productivity. Learn to give up something for another with increased productivity where you will get the best with less amount of time.

Love,
Self.

Dear Self,

Save your energy for something more useful, instead of arguing with someone that refuses to understand or see the truth... just for the sake of arguing and winning. Dwelling long with such a person in an argument can result to throwing insults around and the consequence is not something you might desire. Just walk away for the sake of peace.

Love,

Self.

Dear Self,

If you are going through a terrible situation and people around you can't notice that you are going through a tough time, it shows that you are strong. It is not really easy to appear strong when your whole world is crumbling. If you can find yourself encouraging another person going through difficulties when your situation is worse, you have a strong personality. Keep it up. People will always draw strength from you when they hear your testimony after the storm would have been over. Let this help you stay strong in difficult moments.

Love,

Self.

Dear Self,

Don't be caught talking about someone or saying things, if what you are saying cannot be boldly defended. Most times people you say things to or speak to about someone else, would not always say it exactly how you said it, putting you further into trouble. It is safer not to be known as someone who likes to talk about other people or say things that he or she might likely deny saying when summoned in.

Love,

Self.

Dear Self,

Learn to be independent and responsible. The person you keep asking things from will get tired of you, one day when you least expect it. The person you keep depending on to get things done for you will get tired of your presence tomorrow. Don't be anyone's burden. We all possess greatness - always bet on yourself! And you will win every time.

Love,
Self.

Dear Self,

Don't let your happiness revolve around anyone, you might end up losing yourself if they sever ties with you. You will find yourself in a very devastating position that you never bargained for. Relate with anyone in such a manner that if you lose them, it won't cause you to see the end of life. Don't make anyone be responsible for a part of you that only you can be. Don't expect anything from anyone for you to feel good. Learn to find your happiness yourself, which is usually from within you. Self-Love!

Love,
Self.

Dear YOU,

I love you and we are going to get through this journey called life, TOGETHER! Stay committed to making the necessary changes and surround yourself with love. But, let's love ourselves FIRST! I won't let you down, I will always be here encouraging you through your darkest moments.

Love,

Self.

Dear Self, Daily Affirmations

Transform yourself when in a situation that refuses transformation.

I am transformed to get past my problems.

If you cannot change the situation, change yourself.

I am a work in progress for what I want to achieve in life.

When the situation cannot be changed, I will change to overcome it.

I hold the key to my success; I am the master of my thoughts.

Expect less from people, and get fewer disappointments

I expect little or nothing from anyone, I am not bothered about disappointment

Don't be a liability to anyone. They will get tired of you, someday.

I am not a liability, I am responsible for myself. I am not a burden to anybody.

If people always irritate you, there is something you need to address about you.

I am going to treat every human with respect. There is something special about everyone.

Don't tell someone something you can't stand to defend later.

I would not be found talking about someone if I can't say it to their hearing.

You are strong if your problems hardly show through your countenance.

I am strong enough not to show my problems on my face.

The situation will become a history, someday. Be hopeful.

I am hopeful. I know this situation will one day be in my past, and I will be free again.

You must not have the last word in blind arguments.

I am just going to simply walk away in arguments after making my point clear.

Stop wasting your time by getting too busy doing unproductive things.

I am not interested in getting too busy with doing something unproductive when there are more relevant things to do.

Cry, don't hold back, let those tears drop to help you feel better, then move forward.

I am letting my pain, the bitterness and heaviness go away as each tear drop falls.

Your relevance will be made known by how much you'd be worth, if your pockets are made empty.

I am working on my skills, I don't depend on my money today.

No matter how busy you are, find time to laugh.

I am taking my medicine for today - laughter.

Growth occurs when you accept positive change.

I will improve daily in order to become a better version of Me.

The key to the success you seek lies in your thoughts.

I hold the key to my success; I am the master of my thoughts.

People you encounter are programmed to direct the course of your life, don't neglect it!

I will use the knowledge and experience I gained from my encounter with people for self-improvement. I am learning.

The people you mingle with determine how far you would go in fulfilling your life purpose.

I am conscious of the kind of friends I keep for my progress in life.

Life turbulence are meant to unleash your hidden strengths, not to show your weaknesses.

I will not allow life challenges leave me incapacitated. I will boldly confront them to discover my innate strengths. I am strong.

The best reward for life struggles is not in the accomplishment, but the lesson it taught you.

I will be the best that I can be after each challenge life presents me. I am working myself to greatness.

Until you push harder, you may never discover all your potentials.

I have great potentials. I will push to discover them all. I am great.

Know your worth even when others can't see it.

I know my worth. I am not worthless.

Beyond one's limits lies fear and pain, but persistence and hard work reap good rewards.

I will not allow fear, failure, pain or doubt hinder me from achieving greatness in life. I am pressing on.

When you find your passion, be willing to try your capabilities. It is not going to be easy though.

I am passionate about what I do, and won't give up till I become the best version of myself.

Troubles of life reveal your true strengths and weaknesses. Decide what to do with them.

I am growing stronger and stronger despite life troubles. I see them as opportunity to work on my weaknesses.

Those memories are in the past, don't let them get in the way of your future potentials.

I am not going to allow the events of the past haunt me and get in my way of success. I will keep trying till I make it. Until then, stand clear!

You can hinder yourself from growing when you preoccupy your mind and emotions with feelings of hurt and disappointment from people.

I am not going to allow anyone to control my mind and feelings.

You will forever live in regrets if you deliberately choose to be less than you really are.

I don't belong to the class of mediocrity. I have great potentials and I am working my way to the top with them.

Great people don't compare themselves with others, but with themselves.

The Me in future is my standard. I am less bothered by other people's accomplishments. But always being supportive!

Hold on to the thoughts you have about what you want to do and work towards it on daily basis.

I am doing each day what should be done as planned to help me stay disciplined and organized.

Never give up on a good course.

I am persistent and will not give up on my goals.

Don't fear mistakes, learn from them and correct yourself.

I am not afraid of making mistakes because from them I learn and know what to do right next time.

You'll cut your life short too soon if you work all the time without relaxation.

I work when I should work ,and play when I should play. My life is not out of balance.

It is better to slow down than to quit when you get tired of LIFE. Use your mind to motivate you.

I know how to slow down, and not quit. I am pushing my mind forward no matter how exhausted I am.

Always wear a smile to frustrate life from frustrating you.

I am smiling my way to greatness.

Being tired is a sign that your struggles are almost over.

Though I feel tired, I am not going to give up... now that I am almost at my final destination.

Enjoy friendship with people who like you, and bother less about those that do not.

I can't get emotional because of people that don't like me, especially when I didn't do anything bad to them. I am enjoying my friendships with people that makes me feel important.

You grow smaller when you allow anger to control you, but grow far taller when you choose to forgive.

I am expunging anger from my mind and replacing it with forgiveness to help me become a better person.

It is meaningless to explain when they don't bother to understand you; just remain silent.

I will stop explaining why I said what I said and did what I did. I am standing for myself to guide my feelings of self-worth through silence.

No one is worth taking away your joy.

Nobody deserves taking my joy from me, no matter how close they are to me. I am joyful.

Nobody has the right to judge you if they can not feel exactly how you feel.

You can't feel my pain, I am not bothered with your judgement.

Talk about me, I don't care.

I am busy working on bettering myself, I am not interested in your gossip.

You show strength when you remain humble even with great success.

I am humble, and remain grounded in my values.

Take a deep breath in and out, calm down, think before you react.

I am able to make better decisions when calm before addressing an urgent situation that needs my attention.

Be optimistic and see opportunities. Become pessimistic and see obstacles.

I see opportunities because I am optimistic.

Make someone happy to become happy yourself.

I am happy that I make someone happy.

Don't make hasty decisions when you are emotionally down.

I am waiting till I am in total control of my emotions before I decide on what to do on that matter.

Until you verify the truth, don't believe. Keep quiet.

I am too busy to believe and spread hear-says.

Don't be obsessed with what you don't have, focus on what you have.

I am not going to preoccupy with something I don't have... when I have something I can grow with.

When stuck, use the power of your imagination to find your way forward.

I am using my imaginative power to unlock all doors in my favor.

Life goals are achieved faster than expected when you become the improved version of yourself.

I am SUCCESSFUL!

Becoming a better version of myself prepares me for life's challenges.

I will continue to grow through what I go through...

I am successful; I will use my success to show kindness not arrogance.

I will show others the way to success...

The key to the success you seek lies in your thoughts.

I will remain positive and disassociate myself from anything negative.

Dear Self,_____

_____

_____

_____

_____

_____

_____

_____

_____

_____

_____

_____

_____

_____

_____

_____

_____

_____

_____

_____

_____

Dear Self,_____

Dear Self,_____

_____

_____

_____

_____

_____

_____

_____

_____

_____

_____

_____

_____

_____

_____

_____

_____

_____

_____

_____

_____

Dear Self,

Dear Self,_____

_____

_____

_____

_____

_____

_____

_____

_____

_____

_____

_____

_____

_____

_____

_____

_____

_____

_____

_____

_____

_____

*Dear Self,*_____

_____

_____

_____

_____

_____

_____

_____

_____

_____

_____

_____

_____

_____

_____

_____

_____

_____

_____

_____

_____

_____

_____

*Dear Self,*_____
_____
_____
_____
_____
_____
_____
_____
_____
_____
_____
_____
_____
_____
_____
_____
_____
_____
_____
_____
_____
_____

Dear Self,
_____

_____

_____

_____

_____

_____

_____

_____

_____

_____

_____

_____

_____

_____

_____

_____

_____

_____

_____

_____

_____

_____

_____

_____

_____

_____

Dear Self, _____

_____

_____

_____

_____

_____

_____

_____

_____

_____

_____

_____

_____

_____

_____

_____

_____

_____

_____

_____

_____

_____

_____

Dear Self,_____

_____

_____

_____

_____

_____

_____

_____

_____

_____

_____

_____

_____

_____

_____

_____

_____

_____

_____

_____

_____

_____

_____

*Dear Self,*_____

_____

_____

_____

_____

_____

_____

_____

_____

_____

_____

_____

_____

_____

_____

_____

_____

_____

_____

Dear Self,
_____

_____

_____

_____

_____

_____

_____

_____

_____

_____

_____

_____

_____

_____

_____

_____

_____

_____

_____

_____

_____

*Dear Self,*_____

_____

_____

_____

_____

_____

_____

_____

_____

_____

_____

_____

_____

_____

_____

_____

_____

_____

_____

_____

Dear Self,_____

_____

_____

_____

_____

_____

_____

_____

_____

_____

_____

_____

_____

_____

_____

_____

_____

_____

_____

_____

_____

_____

*Dear Self,*_____

_____

_____

_____

_____

_____

_____

_____

_____

_____

_____

_____

_____

_____

_____

_____

_____

_____

_____

_____

_____

Gigi Roundtree

Dear Self,

*Dear Self,*_____

Dear Self, _____

_____

_____

_____

_____

_____

_____

_____

_____

_____

_____

_____

_____

_____

_____

_____

_____

_____

_____

_____

_____

_____

*Dear Self,*_____

_____

_____

_____

_____

_____

_____

_____

_____

_____

_____

_____

_____

_____

_____

_____

_____

_____

_____

_____

Dear Self,_____

_____

_____

_____

_____

_____

_____

_____

_____

_____

_____

_____

_____

_____

_____

_____

_____

_____

_____

_____

_____

_____

*Dear Self,*_____

_____

_____

_____

_____

_____

_____

_____

_____

_____

_____

_____

_____

_____

_____

_____

_____

_____

_____

Dear Self,
_____

_____

_____

_____

_____

_____

_____

_____

_____

_____

_____

_____

_____

_____

_____

_____

_____

_____

_____

_____

_____

_____

_____

Dear Self,_____

_____

_____

_____

_____

_____

_____

_____

_____

_____

_____

_____

_____

_____

_____

_____

_____

_____

_____

_____

_____

_____

_____

Dear Self,_____

_____

_____

_____

_____

_____

_____

_____

_____

_____

_____

_____

_____

_____

_____

_____

_____

_____

_____

_____

_____

_____

*Dear Self,*_____

_____

_____

_____

_____

_____

_____

_____

_____

_____

_____

_____

_____

_____

_____

_____

_____

_____

_____

_____

_____

_____

_____

_____

Dear Self,

Note to Self

Dear Self,_____

_____

_____

_____

_____

_____

_____

_____

_____

_____

_____

_____

_____

_____

_____

_____

_____

_____

_____

Dear Self,

Note to Self

Dear Self,_____

_____

_____

_____

_____

_____

_____

_____

_____

_____

_____

_____

_____

_____

_____

_____

_____

_____

_____

_____

_____

Dear Self,_____

_____

_____

_____

_____

_____

_____

_____

_____

_____

_____

_____

_____

_____

_____

_____

_____

_____

_____

_____

_____

_____

_____

*Dear Self,*_____

_____

_____

_____

_____

_____

_____

_____

_____

_____

_____

_____

_____

_____

_____

_____

_____

_____

_____

_____

_____

_____

Dear Self,_____

_____

_____

_____

_____

_____

_____

_____

_____

_____

_____

_____

_____

_____

_____

_____

_____

_____

_____

_____

_____

_____

*Dear Self,*_____

_____

_____

_____

_____

_____

_____

_____

_____

_____

_____

_____

_____

_____

_____

_____

_____

_____

_____

_____

_____

_____

Dear Self,_____

_____

_____

_____

_____

_____

_____

_____

_____

_____

_____

_____

_____

_____

_____

_____

_____

_____

_____

_____

_____

_____

_____

_____

Dear Self,_____

_____
_____
_____
_____
_____
_____
_____
_____
_____
_____
_____
_____
_____
_____
_____
_____
_____
_____
_____
_____

Dear Self,

Dear Self,_____

_____

_____

_____

_____

_____

_____

_____

_____

_____

_____

_____

_____

_____

_____

_____

_____

_____

_____

Dear Self,_____

Note to Self

Dear Self,_____

_____

_____

_____

_____

_____

_____

_____

_____

_____

_____

_____

_____

_____

_____

_____

_____

_____

_____

_____

_____

_____

Gigi Roundtree

Dear Self,_____

_____

_____

_____

_____

_____

_____

_____

_____

_____

_____

_____

_____

_____

_____

_____

_____

_____

_____

_____

80155163R10086

Made in the USA
San Bernardino, CA
25 June 2018